A Little, a Mime, a Pool of Slime

More about Nouns

To Noreen
—B.P.C.

Noun: A word that names a person, animal, place, or thing

A Lime, a Mime, a Pool of Slime

More about Nouns

by Brian P Cleary

illustrated by Brian Gable

LERNER BOOKS · LONDON · NEW YORK · MINNEAPOLIS

A jet is a noun,

and so is Peru.

4

Friend is a noun, and so is your dad,

ice cream
and bagels
and Boston

QUINCY MARKET

and Brad.

If it's a hippo, house, or ham,

if it's your coach, cockroach, or ram,

if it's a rock,

clock, or clown,

then—oh my gosh, Josh—
it's a noun!

9

And so is your grandma and baby llama, a billy goat, and big red comma,

COMMA

a doorway, Norway,
hand-me-downs—
all the things you see
are nouns.

If it's a person,
place,
or thing,
a palace,
pal,

or shiny bling,

12

a shack or sheriff
in your town,

it's fundamental—
it's a noun!

But there are nouns
you cannot touch
or smell or hear or see.

This type is called an
abstract noun,
like joy and harmony.

Love and hate are
abstract nouns,
and so are peace and hope.

You cannot taste or hold them,
like a tart or telescope.

Proper nouns
all name specific
people, things, and places.

Like Uncle Lou

or Timbuktu,

they start with upper cases.

Like Mallory or Valerie, the Seventeenth Street Gallery,

Pizza Pete's and Ming's Chinese,

proper nouns name each of these.

Or Brannigan
and Flannigan,
parading in
with Anne again.

Whether they're **abstract** or proper or neither,

whether it's talent or Timmy or teether,

if it can be thought about,

ridden to town,

talked to, or walked to,
it's surely a noun!

Like beagle
or eagle,
a robin
or wren,

A lime,

a mime,

a pool

of slime,

a breeze,
a sneeze,
a scary mime.

Nouns are words like
girls and curls,
cats and flats,

FLATS

HEELS

and hats
and pearls.

A crumb, some gum,
a tiny rocket—

a noun can be
what's in your pocket.

If it's a **tape** or DVD,

a teacher's aide or Germany,

a coat that's made of

wool
or down,

then say it with me—
it's a noun!

So, what is a noun?

Do you know?

About the Author & Illustrator

Brian P Cleary is the author of the best-selling Words Are CATegorical® series, as well as the Math Is CATegorical®, Sounds Like Reading™, and Adventures in Memory™ series, The Laugh Stand: Adventures in Humor, Peanut Butter and Jellyfishes: A Very Silly Alphabet Book, Rainbow Soup: Adventures in Poetry, and Rhyme & PUNishment: Adventures in Wordplay. Mr. Cleary lives in Cleveland, Ohio, USA.

Brian Gable is the illustrator of several Words Are CATegorical® books, as well as the Math Is CATegorical® series. Mr. Gable also works as a political cartoonist for the Globe and Mail newspaper in Toronto, Canada.

Text copyright © 2006 by Brian P Cleary
Illustrations copyright © 2006 by Lerner Publishing Group, Inc.

First published in the United States of America in 2008

First published in the United Kingdom in 2010 by
Lerner Books,
Dalton House,
60 Windsor Avenue,
London SW19 2RR

Website address: www.lernerbooks.co.uk

British Library Cataloguing in Publication Data

Cleary, Brian P., 1959-
  A lime, a mime, a pool of slime : more about nouns.
  1. English language—Noun—Juvenile poetry.
  I. Title
  425.5-dc22

ISBN-13: 978 0 7613 5400 0

Printed in China